I0199473

HEAVENLY

Waters

Mikvah Messages for Our Daily Lives

BY MIRIAM YERUSHALMI

Heavenly Waters: Mikvah Messages for Our Daily Lives

ISBN: 978-0-578-44571-7
Second Edition - Shevat 5779 / January 2019

Copyright © 2019 by Miriam Yerushalmi

All rights reserved. No part of this book may be reproduced in
any form without written permission from the copyright holder.

Printed in the USA by Jewish Girls Unite - www.jewishgirlsunite.com

Design & Layout by Carasmatic Design - www.CarasmaticDesign.com

לעילוי נשמת

My dear mother-in-law and father-in-law
Leah bas Avraham
Yisrael Avraham ben Moshe

My dear Grandma
Esther bas Miriam

My dear uncle Shmuel ben Benieyahu

My dear aunt Sara bas Benieyahu

לעילוי נשמת

Yehudah Aryeh Leon HaKohen
ben Kochavah Stella

by his Loving Wife & Children

Cohen, Benmor, Liniado
& Altahleff families

*In loving memory of the parents of
my dear friend Dr. Carole Lerman*

Leah bat Betzalel HaKohen z"l

*Shraga Feivel Hersch ben
Yisroel Yechiel z"l*

Much gratitude and sincere appreciation to

Jason Zaiderman
and family

*for their contributions over the years that
help projects like these come to fruition.*

*May G-d continue to bless the whole family
for generations to come.*

In honor of my dear friend Esther Abeniem's parents

Gittel bas Esther

&

Reuven ben Fruma Etta

In honor of my dear friend Aliza Elkayam's parents and in-laws

אברהם בן יצחק

שרה פיגה בת משה

ראבן בן אליהו

סלטנה שושנה בת יחיאי

Thank you Shoshana and Ephraim Bander

for your continuous donations to SANE that help people in crises and help prevent crises!

In loving memory of

Mrs. Freida and
Mr. Efrayim Blum

and their sons

David ben Efrayim
& Danny ben Efrayim

TABLE OF CONTENTS

It is the duty of wives and daughters (may they live and be well) to stand in the first rank of every activity dedicated to strengthening religion and Judaism in general, particularly concerning Taharat Hamishpacha (laws of family purity). They must organize a Society of Daughters to reinforce all the Chassidic practices concerning upbringing and education of children.

-Hayom Yom, 21 Shvat

Dedication

This book is dedicated to my dear mother Esther and my father Gabriel Levy, for their *mesiras nefesh* to ensure I had a Jewish education; to my children Yechezkal Moshe and Chana Leah, my wonderful assistants, the ultimate catalysts for my personal development, whose presence in my life has motivated me to search for the deepest truths to become the best I can be so as to help others become their best selves.

Thank you especially to my dear husband, the other half of my soul, David Yerushalmi — to paraphrase Rabbi Akiva, "Everything that is mine, is his." He has always believed in me and always supported me in all my projects, in every way: financially and emotionally. He works tirelessly on behalf of the Jewish people and is a true Maccabee of this generation. May *Hashem* bless him in everything.

To my dear Lubavitcher Rebbe, Rabbi Menachem Mendel Schneerson, for all his *mesiras nefesh*, who continues to pave the way anew with his life's work.

Ultimately, I owe my thanks to *Hashem* for His care and His kindness, for leading me to Torah and opening my heart to the inner dimensions of *Chassidus*.

INTRODUCTION

The information in this book is meant to help women fully benefit from the Mikvah experience, and at the same time to strengthen and better the marriage. As the Lubavitcher Rebbe often said, "Good is good, but better is better."

Marriage can be as holy as a "devouring fire," full of fervor, passion and enthusiasm. Each partner can connect with the other and become attached with a bond so strong, with feelings of love for one another, that their unity creates within them the most eternal peace on earth. This true love experience ignites a soul ascent. Husband and wife unify with each other wherever they may be, near or far, always close in heart and soul. Together they are able to conquer worlds, to make an abode for Divinity here on earth; to build a true Jewish home; a miniature sanctuary of their own out of their beautiful love.

The intimate relationship between a husband and a wife mirrors the union between G-d and the Jewish people. Each person has been given the unique power to feel oneness with G-d. By examining the marital relationship, we find the proper means to approach the Divine. Understanding the Mikvah experience and laws can serve as a practical guide to preparing the physical body to live in true unity with the soul, a part of G-d. Each *halacha* in the preparation for Mikvah immersion can be understood as a secret message teaching us how to refine and purify ourselves spiritually, as well as offer us practical tools to overcome the inner struggles we face in our daily lives.

Throughout this process, a woman invites the love of her husband, as well as the infinite love of the Divine which permeates the marital relationship and the entire home atmosphere. When we strengthen ourselves, we strengthen the entire family.

As Jewish women, let's realize the awesomeness of the holy task that has been placed upon our shoulders: to be the guarantors for the future of the entire Jewish people.

Dear Jewish Woman,

The laws of Mikvah purification are like a user manual which gives us the ability to maximize the potential of a product. G-d created marriage, and He also created the "manual" for marriage. Although the laws of purity and impurity belong to a category of *mitzvot* known as *chukim*, Divine decrees, for which no reason is given, Mikvah enhances and elevates the marital relationship, especially intimacy. There is a four stage process in the observance of Family Purity: separation, preparation, sanctification and renewed connection with one's spouse on the Mikvah night. A woman follows the laws of Mikvah with the intention of fulfilling them as best as possible. By fulfilling the *halacha*, the Torah confers upon us multiple layers of reward and enrichment. The goal of this book is to provide you with deep insights, reflections, and meditations that will enhance the performance of the Mikvah ritual with sound mind, body and soul.

For the past thirty years, I have studied the laws of Mikvah and have been awed by their depth and beauty. Every instance of studying these laws revealed another layer of meaning that impacted my Mikvah experience, and I wanted others to benefit from my realizations. As a counselor, I wanted to give women the opportunity to appreciate the Divine experience of Mikvah night on a deeper level, and prepare not only physically, but also emotionally and spiritually. In the Mikvah preparation chapter we present the *halacha*, followed by soul and mind reflections that connect to the physical preparation. I believe that these laws are a blueprint with spiritual messages for daily life. **One is not required by Jewish law to incorporate any of these reflections into the Mikvah ritual.** The ideas presented in this book are a means to maximize the *mitzvah* from a holistic perspective: symbolically and metaphorically. **This book is not an all-inclusive Taharat Hamishpacha guidebook with all the details of the laws.**

Consider this your helpful guidebook as you embark upon your journey to strengthen your marital relationship and achieve greater levels of love for yourself, your spouse, and G-d.

I invite you to use these reflections to enhance your Mikvah experience emotionally, psychologically, and spiritually and apply whatever may seem meaningful to you. You may find that these concepts are still relevant for your personal growth after the Mikvah years have concluded.

I encourage you to read these ideas and reflections at a time when you are relaxed and not rushed. As you reflect, envision yourself performing the physical preparations for Mikvah. When you read the mind and soul part of the *mitzvah*, remember that this is where I added my own analogous connections to offer you the opportunity to enhance your own personal experience. The description of the symbolism of the actual Mikvah structure is an idea that I pondered a great deal. It reminded me of our journey on this earth to purify our natural tendencies, in the same way the rain waters purify the tap waters in the Mikvah. The *kavanot* (intentions or meditations) one can have while intimate are based on *Kabbalistic* teachings as taught by Rabbi Yitzchak Ginsburgh, taken from his book *Mystery of Marriage*, pages 331-356.

The Mikvah meditations and concepts presented in this book are designed to open your heart to give and receive the love you deserve in marriage. The goal is to infuse the physical actions of the *mitzvah* with the intentions that will penetrate your mind and heart and make it easy to sustain a loving and harmonious relationship. I pray that as you read this book you will appreciate the holiness in yourself and in your spouse, and that you experience happiness all the days of your lives, forever together, reaching new heights through the heavenly waters of Mikvah.

Sincerely,

Miriam Yerushalmi

CHAPTER ONE

MIKVAH REFLECTIONS

What is a Mikvah?

Mikvah means "collection." A Mikvah, ritual bath, is a pool that collects natural water from rain, a river or an underground spring untouched by human hands. Though a Mikvah looks something like a small pool or bath, it is a truly spiritual tool rather than an entity connected to personal hygiene. In fact, a user must be physically clean prior to immersion. Jews — men and women alike — immerse in the Mikvah prior to engaging in certain ritual acts.

In the practice of family purity, the woman immerses following a period of physical separation from her husband that had commenced with the onset of menstruation. On the eve of the night the couple is to resume relations, the wife enters the waters of the Mikvah, where she says a prayer inviting G-d to sanctify her forthcoming intimacy with her husband. Her immersion marks the start of renewed physical intimacy between husband and wife. This phase of the relationship lasts until the start of her next period.

Heavenly Waters

A conscious effort is required to achieve *shalom bayit*, a loving and harmonious relationship in marriage. By the time one has reached marriageable age, each individual has a unique past and set of life experiences, not to mention distinct likes and dislikes. Fortunately, Jewish marriage itself provides tools for reconciling the divergent backgrounds of husband and wife without promoting

The waters of Mikvah have the potential to renew, refresh and confer a sense of new beginning, reminiscent of the world at its very birth.

loss of individual identity. One such tool is the practice of Family Purity, with the Mikvah as its centerpiece, which is a G-d-given gift that belongs to every Jewish woman. Historically, Mikvah has played a critical role in Jewish life, so much so that when a community lacks both a Mikvah and a synagogue, its members must first build a Mikvah. The practice of family purity provides stability and richness for the Jewish home and family. After visiting the Mikvah a Jewish woman imbues her marriage with holiness and a feeling of harmony.

A Mikvah is a "ritual bath of living waters," for it is used to re-attain ritual purity or to ascend to a higher level of purity. Jewish law requires that one immerse in a Mikvah as part of the process of conversion to Judaism. Before dishes and utensils can be used in a kosher kitchen, they must acquire an additional measure of holiness which is conferred through the ritual immersion in a Mikvah. Some men have the custom to immerse every day in the Mikvah, and others immerse as a preparation for *Shabbat*.

We can understand the significance of Mikvah by examining the spiritual potential of water itself. According to the Torah, water filled the world in the first stage of creation. Genesis 1:2 reads, "...when the earth was astonishingly empty, with darkness upon the surface of the deep, and the Divine Presence hovered upon the surface of the waters..." In connection with the primordial character of water, the waters of a Mikvah at their time of collection resemble the original waters of creation. This symbolism dovetails with Jewish law's mandate that the source of Mikvah waters is derived from a rainfall or from an underground source.

The waters of Mikvah have the potential to renew, refresh and confer a sense of new beginning, reminiscent of the world at its very birth. When a woman visits the Mikvah, in a sense, she emerges from the water and starts fresh, unencumbered by past obstacles to her personal growth and life mission.

A Time for Growth

The word Mikvah can also be translated as a place of *"kaveh,"* "hope." Within the womb of the Mikvah, we nurture the hope that we will emerge anew. Immersion in Mikvah inspires us with hope to continue growing

and reaching toward our higher potential, instead of remaining stagnant in life. When one expresses hope, one is considered righteous, since even in the midst of a negative occurrence, one recognizes the opportunity for growth that is always present. As a result, one can redirect one's life and bring salvation and transformation.

The flowing waters symbolize movement and change as they are in constant motion. In a similar vein, regarding matters of purity, a movement towards growth is the key determining factor. It is through these "currents" that one can foster hope of evolving, advancing and becoming one's purest self. Through continually striving to grow, one can maintain a constant, vibrant and renewed connection not only with oneself, but also with one's spouse, and G-d. When we purify ourselves by immersing in a Mikvah, we take on the spiritual qualities of those holy flowing waters.

What is the significance of traversing from a state of impurity to purity?

Chassidus teaches, "Every descent is for the purpose of a greater ascent." The world also goes through a weekly cycle, with six days of mundane activity leading up to the heightened spiritual experience of *Shabbat*. After *Shabbat*, it is necessary to return to the spiritual "low" of the work week, in order to prepare for an even higher spiritual elevation the following *Shabbat*. The more effort is put into preparing for the holy day, the more of a rewarding experience it becomes.

The same is true of a woman's monthly cycle. Her state of impurity gives her the opportunity to work towards an even higher level of transformation and self-actualization each month. The *mitzvah* of Mikvah gives a woman the gift of constant renewal, giving her a spiritual "high" and heightened Divine awareness.

Relax and feel secure knowing that your bond is sacred.
You and your partner are made perfectly for each other.

At the time of immersion in the Mikvah, you receive an extra measure of strength to deepen your connection with *Hashem* and your husband. Believe that *Hashem* is with you in every detail of your life and is directing your steps to a more refined destiny. Be patient with yourself while you strengthen yourself and your marriage. Challenges exist to bring out your highest potential. Your efforts to keep the *mitzvah* of *shalom bayit* are profoundly meaningful to *Hashem*.

These laws are called *Family* Purity because your commitment to this *mitzvah* brings blessings and benefits to your whole family.

"An attitude of gratitude" will keep you focused on the joy. Recognize that everything you have is a gift from *Hashem*. Regardless of the size of your bank account, you and your partner have many simple pleasures in life to share.

Relax and feel secure knowing that your bond is sacred. You and your partner are made perfectly for each other.

CHAPTER TWO

MIKVAH PREPARATIONS

Mikvah Preparation Checklist

- Take a bath (for at least ½ hour), wash all areas and all hair
- Shower and wash hair with shampoo (preferably without conditioner)
- Comb all hair very well while wet to remove all knots
- Shower and comb again at the mikvah if a bath was taken at home
- Cut finger and toe nails to the tips. Check around nails for hanging skin.

Remove...

- Jewelry
- Bandages, band-aids and sticky substances
- Contact lenses
- Make-up (lipstick, face and eye make-up including mascara and all traces of remover)
- Nail polish
- Scabs that come off easily
- Dentures, false teeth
- Splinters
- Deodorant
- Any foreign object or dirt

Clean...

- Eyes
- Nose
- Ears and earring holes
- Teeth: brush and remove all particles between teeth and rinse mouth
- Between fingers and toes
- Navel
- Around all nails
- Body surfaces and folds

- Use restroom if necessary
- Soften scabs and calluses. Keep soft until attendant arrives.
- If you use the bathroom, rewash and re-comb the area.
- Do a final inspection of your body for intervening substances, and convey any uncertainties to the Mikvah attendant.
- Do not dry yourself. Put on a robe and slippers and let the Mikvah attendant know that you are ready for immersion.

Integrating Mind, Body and Soul

How do we make the most of the Mikvah night? How do we achieve a spiritual victory of our pure soul over the natural base tendencies and strengthen marital love and *shalom bayit*?

Preparations for immersion in the Mikvah are the guidelines to self-sanctification and purification not only of the body, but of the soul; they constitute the necessary preparation for unification with G-d. The steps in the Mikvah purification process are all reminders and tools to purify and transform the daily interactions between husband and wife. A woman's monthly dip in the Mikvah is an opportunity to pamper the body, mind and soul.

Following the laws delineated in the book *Family Purity* by Rabbi Fishel Jacobs, we will view each law symbolically and metaphorically as a reminder of the internal work necessary to refine our conduct and patterns of behavior when relating to our spouse. In addition, understanding the connection between the physical and spiritual meanings of the Mikvah experience will help us connect our mind and heart to the Divine and enable us to feel the *kedushah*, holiness and sacred bond that we create through this unique *mitzvah*.

Welcome to this awesome journey for the mind, body and soul.

Before Mikvah Preparations Begin

body The preparations for Mikvah immersion actually begin a week before Mikvah night. Shortly before sunset, on the day her period ends (at least the fifth day of menstrual cycle), a woman makes the initial internal examination (*Hefsek Tahara*) using a soft white checking cloth. For the following seven days, she wears white undergarments and uses white bed linens. She performs daily *bedikos* in the morning and evening to make sure that no bleeding or staining has occurred. Immersion takes place the following week, after nightfall, on the same day of the week as the initial examination. (For example, if she makes the initial examination on Sunday before sunset, she will immerse on the following Sunday night.)

soul Rabbi Samson ben Tzadok, student of the *Maharam* of Rothenberg, writes that "all customs pertaining to a *chatan* and *kallah* (groom and bride) are derived from the giving of the Torah, where *Hashem* revealed Himself as the *chatan* towards the *kallah* — *Klal Yisrael*."

Just like the Jewish people counted 49 (7x7) days in anticipation for receiving the Torah on Mount Sinai, a woman counts 7 days to reunite with her husband. Through the couple's love for G-d, and by uniting with one another in love, they arouse G-d's love for them.

mind The Mikvah night is likened to the wedding night — a fresh start to rekindle the love and connection between a couple. The Talmud says, "she separates so she may become as beloved to her husband on the day of her immersion as on the first day of marriage." Absence makes the heart grow fonder.

One of the possible causes of marital distress is dissatisfaction in intimate life. The laws of Mikvah keep the spark alive. The Kinsey Institute study shows that the highest frequency for relations in people over age 35 is by observant Jews. A 1998 Brandeis University study revealed that the most enduring marriages are of Mikvah users: 52% of marriages fail, whereas only 1.2% of Mikvah-observant marriages fail.

Reflect:

- As you count the seven days to Mikvah night, remember counting the days towards your wedding. The white linen and garments are a reminder of your white bridal gown.

- Recall the moments on your wedding day that changed your lives forever.

- What have you accomplished together as a couple?

1. Prepare Joyfully

body *Halacha:* Every minuscule detail in preparing for the Mikvah is important. However, this can lead to feeling stressed because of all the myriad details involved. How do we ensure that our meticulousness does not interfere with the joy of the *mitzvah*? It is essential to have adequate time to prepare so that you are not forced to go through the motions in a rush. It may be a good idea to make arrangements to arrive at the Mikvah a little earlier and find a babysitter, if necessary. When you are less rushed you can achieve a new level of appreciation and *kavanah* in your Mikvah observance. Your physical preparations will become the time to purify both externally and internally, inside and out.

soul Mikvah preparation can be applied to the spiritual preparations necessary for every *mitzvah* we do. If preparing for *Shabbat* or holidays feels overwhelming, you can overcome the stress, through meditating on the concept that your soul is uniting with *Hashem* through every *mitzvah*. When we infuse joy and an aura of calm into our actions, we spread the joy of the *mitzvot* to our family.

Note that some women may not realize that their repetitive checking, scrubbing, or washing may actually indicate an obsessive-compulsive disorder, which may require professional help. (See appendix on page 100.)

mind Take some time to contemplate the bigger picture and remember that you are preparing to perform a *mitzvah* as significant as circumcision and fasting on *Yom Kippur*. You are a link in a powerful chain connecting you to all Jewish women throughout history starting from our Matriarchs Sarah, Rivkah, Rachel, and Leah.

You can approach the Mikvah preparations with joy and calm by cultivating positive thoughts about your spouse. As your thoughts generate feelings of joy and gratitude, you will actually look forward to immersion.

Reflect:

- Recall a precious and happy memory of a wonderful time spent together.

- What are you grateful for today in your marriage?

- Recite an affirmation such as, "I am blessed to have a husband." Some women are still waiting to find their partner.

2. Check for Barriers

body *Halacha:* One must inspect the body for any dough and ensure that it doesn't obstruct the water from reaching all places. A woman looks into the mirror to make sure that her face is clean and her makeup is removed.

soul The reference to dough may also symbolize *chametz*, which is likened to arrogance according to *Chassidus*. Arrogance, like *chametz*, rises and proliferates. We make space for others by ridding ourselves of arrogance. We can be open to understanding another person's feelings and perspective, even if different from our own. Empathy and understanding are vital ingredients in a happy marriage. In addition, through humility, we create space for G-d in our lives.

mind Look in the mirror. What do you see? Are you smiling? Does your body language and the nuances of your voice and behavior spread love and positivity?

Non-verbal communication can be more powerful than words. The shape of our lips or the furrow of our brows can mean a great deal. As we get to know our spouse better, we become more aware of how the subtleties of self-expression, the innuendos, and gestures, carry messages as potent as words and conversations themselves.

Remember that joy and positivity are contagious, and even if at times it may be hard, a woman sets the tone in the relationship. When a man knows his wife is happy, he is happy.

Reflect:

- Look in the mirror and tell yourself: "I am beautiful on the inside and outside."
- Believe that you are beautiful, attractive, unique and special.
- Believe that you are loving, caring, kind and positive.

3. Remove Barriers

body *Halacha:* Close to the time of immersion, a woman scrubs her body and combs her hair thoroughly to ensure there are no intervening substances. Any foreign object found on a woman's body may invalidate the immersion.

soul Mikvah is compared to the womb, which is completely pure. A Mikvah requires a measurement of 40 *se'ah*, a unit of ancient origin used in Jewish law, just like there are 40 weeks of gestation and 40 days for an embryo to take on human form. The experience of purity through the Mikvah is an experience of rebirth. It helps foster forgiveness with an open heart. When we relinquish any past hurts, we welcome a flow of renewal in our lives and relationships.

mind How can you remove any barriers that may be blocking you from a deeper connection with your spouse? Take a quiet moment to cultivate forgiveness in your heart.

Your husband can sense when he has been forgiven, and during that moment your relationship is created anew. This is an auspicious time to start all over again. Mikvah night is your time to become one again with your partner, physically, emotionally, and spiritually. We are one in body, mind and soul.

Relationships are built moment by moment. Each time we judge favorably and save the moment, we steer our relationship in the right direction and become truly one.

Reflect:

- How can you judge your husband favorably?

4. Cut the Nails

body *Halacha:* A woman must cut and file her finger and toenails as a preparation for Mikvah.

soul The *Hayom Yom* compares the fingernails to harsh criticism or rebuke. One must pare one's own fingernails in order not to gash the other.

Likewise, when we do need to rebuke or criticize someone, we need to make sure that our words will not "scratch" or hurt the other person.

A common tendency is to project our own faults onto others. But not only our faults; it is also easy to project our desire for self-improvement onto another. "He's got to work on himself." We truly desire to improve our relationship, so we demand that the other person changes his behavior. We believe that our relationship can only improve if he changes. In this way, we do not feel the need to make any efforts to better our own conduct.

The first step in "cutting one's nails" is to look at the person we seek to criticize with his benefit in mind. The sole goal of offering reproof should be his self-improvement. This will help us find loving and creative ways to administer it, so that our words will be received well.

mind It cannot be stressed enough that words are tremendously powerful, especially when spoken to those closest to us. As wives, we can tap into our ability to use the art of gentle persuasion in communication, to encourage our spouse through love and positive words of affirmation, instead of criticism using words or facial expressions. As a result, we will create a peaceful, warm and loving environment.

Be honest with yourself and examine your faults in a positive and uplifting way by recognizing your mastery over your thoughts, speech, and actions.

Reflect:

- Does my constructive criticism come from a place of love and respect?
- Are there areas I can work on to improve myself, instead of trying to change my spouse?

5. Use Hot Water

body *Halacha:* Hot water should be used for washing and bathing. If only limited hot water is available, then the hair should be washed and combed first. Cold water tends to stiffen the hair strands, making hair less manageable and harder to detangle.

soul Hot water symbolizes a fiery love and passion. Rabbi Akiva taught that the Hebrew word for man is "*ish*", spelled *aleph, yud, shin.* Remove the *yud* and you have *aleph, shin* or *esh*, meaning fire. The Hebrew word for woman is "*ishah*", spelled *aleph, shin, hei.* Remove the *hei* and once again, you have *esh*, meaning fire.

This teaches us that there is a consuming fire in the heart of every man and woman. If husband and wife do not make the Divine Presence (symbolized by *yud* and *hei*) welcome, they are left with two consuming fires. When the fire of man and woman connect in a worthy way, you have the fire of G-d. When G-d's presence dwells in a marriage, the fire gives warmth and passionate love, and brings Divine blessing into their lives.

In the *Shema* prayer, we are commanded to love G-d. How can we be commanded to love? The commandment to love G-d is an obligation on our part to reflect upon and appreciate G-d's kindness to us. *Shema*, means not only hear, but understand. The more we think that we owe everything to G-d: our lives, our health, our family, our homes, our being able to think, speak, walk, the sunshine, the very air we breathe — and how everything is a free gift from our benevolent G-d, then surely we could not help but love Him!

Our daily prayers do not begin immediately with the *Shema*. There is a great deal to say and to think before we come to *Shema*, so that by the time we come to the *Shema* G-d is no longer a "stranger" to us.

mind Reflecting on G-d's kindness arouses a person's passionate love for G-d. The more a person yearns with a passion for G-d, the more one desires to transmit this love to one's soulmate. Through experiencing G-d's closeness and embrace, a person will be able to tolerate the imperfections in the other and will avoid being distant and cold. A person with love for *Hashem* will overflow with warmth and compassion for others.

Reflect:

- How can I express my love for G-d?
- When do I feel G-d's love for me?
- How does my love for G-d enhance my marriage?

6. Wash the Body

body

Halacha: We prepare for immersion by cleansing our flesh and washing away any dirt. We wear fresh "garments."

soul

While we wash and cleanse ourselves, we can also use this time to wash away negative thoughts, speech, and actions that may create tension in the marriage and home. Stains can be viewed metaphorically as our own negative tendencies that can damage relationships, such as speaking rudely or "putting him in his place because he deserves it." Instinctual habits and negative reactions arise from our animal soul. The physical preparations open up the channels to wash away unhealthy habits. We cleanse ourselves and purify our thoughts, speech, and actions.

Allowing negativity to fester places additional blockages not only between the two parties but between the person and G-d, as well. By practicing tolerance and compassion and refraining from sinking into compelling feelings of hostility or vengefulness, we let our soul shine. We clothe our soul in sacred new spiritual garments: holy thoughts, speech, and actions. Thus we create a vessel to receive G-d's blessings.

mind We want to ensure that our communication reflects love and kindness because these are the messages that ultimately create peace and harmony in a relationship. For the sake of peace, be determined to avoid reacting to everything that a spouse says and taking another person's negativity to heart.

It is vital to remind ourselves, again and again, to keep our attitude and thoughts in a receptive and loving mode. The following self-reflective questions can also help ensure that our thoughts, speech, and actions create a loving bond.

Reflect:

- What thoughts do I choose to think about my husband?

- Do my words reflect love and acceptance of my spouse? What can I say to verbalize respect for my husband? Do I express words of praise and gratitude?

- What can I do to improve and enhance our relationship?

- Is my negative reaction, which may be justified, interfering with our bond?

7. Scrub and Cleanse

body

Halacha: The woman washes and scrubs her body thoroughly with soap and cleansing agents to remove any dirt or external substances.

soul

The most powerful way to rid the psyche of unwanted "baggage" or unnecessary "toxic" emotions is through the study of the inner dimension of Torah, otherwise known as *Chassidus*. These teachings are a most powerful cleansing agent. Women and men both need the fortification of *Kabbalah*. Now more than ever, (says the Lubavitcher Rebbe, quoted in the *Gutnick Chumash*) women need to study the deepest parts of Torah because they are exposed to the "marketplace" of secularism. We are all confronted with many concepts antithetical to Torah values.

Set aside a few minutes daily to study the teachings from our Holy Chassidic Masters and feed your soul. Resources are available on TorahCafe.com and Chabad.org.

Miriam Yerushalmi's lectures can be found on Youtube and TorahAnytime.com. Her books are: *Reaching New Heights through Kindness in Marriage*, *Reaching New Heights through Prayer and Meditation* and *Reaching New Heights through Health and Happiness*.

mind Use powerful tools of visualization and meditation to remove negative thoughts that may interfere with positive emotions in your marriage. Use the guided meditations in this book.

Take deep, regular breaths until you are breathing in a steady rhythm. With each inhalation, visualize that you are breathing in everything that is good: tranquility, love, harmony, and optimism. With each exhalation, breathe out everything that is troublesome: tension, sadness, bitterness, anger, and pessimism. Feel lighter, as a soothing wave of relaxation flows over and through you.

- Meditate on a Torah thought and how you can apply it to your life.

8. Wash in All Places

body — *Halacha:* The areas between the toes, the armpits and between layers of fat need to be thoroughly washed.

soul — Torah compares fat to physical pleasures (*Likkutei Torah*). True pleasure is generated when one spouse values the other for their genuine character, for their admiration and acceptance of him or her, and for their kindness and fear of G-d. It is important to look beyond the pleasures in life, to make a mental note of what is not important, and to see where excess is getting in the way of appreciation.

When a husband feels that he is under pressure to provide more for his wife and is under-appreciated for what he is already doing, he loses strength to continue at his pace and does not perform as well in his work. Furthermore, he may lose his emotional desire for his wife and fall short in satisfying her emotionally and in areas of intimacy, as well.

mind It is so important to appreciate your spouse for his true qualities rather than what he provides for you materially. How many "big" comforts and extra things are necessary to make a person happy? Research shows that the margin of happiness does not increase based on "items" or accumulated disposable wealth beyond very basic needs.

Greed and selfishness can destroy a marriage. A woman can get trapped in the need to keep up with her friends. It all starts with a feeling that one must have more clothes, a larger home, and a more expensive car, but ultimately the list becomes endless and can be destructive.

Reflect:

- Am I satisfied and grateful for my blessings, or do my desires for excess needs and luxuries get in the way of my true happiness?

- Start a gratitude journal and list the small things that make a big difference in your life.

9. Check the "Invisible"

body *Halacha:* The Biblical requirement is to inspect the body for any obstructions to the Mikvah waters prior to immersion. A woman examines her entire body to ensure that she has removed any intervening substances. Intervening substances may include stains, facial makeup, nail polish, loose hairs on the back, dough, and anything obstructing the water from reaching the skin. The parts of the body that are not visible to the eye should be checked with her hands and with a mirror. Check the blind spots on the back for loose hairs. This process is called *bedika,* or inspection.

soul World-renowned *Kabbalah* lecturer, Rabbi Laibl Wolf says that Kabbalah describes angels as the "offspring" of thoughts. A negative thought about another actually creates a "bad angel," whereas a "good angel" is created when we think a positive thought. The angels created with our thoughts about another hover around us. Have you ever felt a negative static or sense of tension that can be described as "a heaviness so thick you can cut it with a knife"? We cannot entirely fault the other person for the heavy feeling; we are responsible, too. When we are in contact with someone whom we had previously thought negatively about, there is a confluence of negative energies. The person intuitively picks up on our negativity, and the relationship may become distant and cold.

Just as we examine the hard-to-reach places, Mikvah provides us with an opportunity to examine and let go of hidden negative thoughts and transform them into positive thoughts. As a result, we remove the barriers to our soul so the "negative angels" melt away.

mind The *Ramban* writes in his letter to his son, "Review your actions every morning and evening, and in this way live all your days in repentance."

Reflect:

- What are the intervening "substances" to my healthy marriage? What are my spiritual blockages to a wholesome relationship?

- How can I reframe negative thoughts to a positive thought and create a good angel?

- Do I let go of the "sticky" thoughts and reframe them to focus on the blessings in life?

10. Heart and Sole

body *Halacha:* In a final check-up on the way to the *Mikvah,* we take extra caution in order to be free of the smallest speck of dirt, even on the toes. After walking from the shower to the Mikvah, she checks the bottoms of her feet again to ensure that no dirt is stuck to them and, if necessary, rinses them off. After the *bedika,* a woman is careful not to come into contact with any dirt or sticky substances.

soul Checking the soles of the feet remind us of an important lesson for daily life. Feet are at the lowest point of the body but lead the head to its destination. At the end of the day, our actions are what count. The Sages explain, *"Hama'aseh hu haikar"* (the deed is the main thing). It is what we do which matters most.

A woman's wisdom and kindness are expressed through her actions and *mitzvot.* As the psychological bedrock of the home, a woman sets the tone, mood and emotional tempo of the home. Through fulfilling G-d's commandment, even the smallest ones, she welcomes the Divine presence and creates a sanctuary for G-d.

mind The Kotzker Rebbe asked his students, "Where is G-d"? He answered, "Wherever you let Him in." We invite G-d into our dining room when we light the *Shabbat* candles, and into our kitchen when we prepare Kosher food. Through Mikvah, we allow G-d into our bedroom, making it holy. The master bedroom is referred to as "the Holy of Holies." Our union is compared to the *Kohen Gadol* (High Priest) entering the Holy of Holies. Just as after immersion, the High Priest entered the Holy of Holies, so too after Mikvah, husband and wife enter their "Holy of Holies"- their bedroom.

The triangle is the strongest structure. With *Hashem* as an invested third Partner we have every chance to succeed at a long-lasting fulfilling marriage.

Reflect:

- What action do I take to care for my home, my sanctuary with joy?

- What can I do to invite G-d into every room in my home?

- Do I complain about my responsibilities or do I realize that my children are a treasured gift from G-d? How do I express my gratitude to G-d and my family? If I can maintain this positive awareness about my children, I can do the same for my spouse.

My Reflections:

....
....
....
....
....
....
....
....
....
....
....
....
....
....
....
....
....
....

CHAPTER THREE

MIKVAH IMMERSION

A Spa for the Soul

body *Halacha:* Immersion in the Mikvah is the culmination of the purification process. The body must be completely submerged in the water, from head to toe. The minimum amount of water that must be present in a Mikvah, through which a person becomes spiritually "reborn," is 40 *se'ah*. This is the quantity necessary to ensure that the entire body is immersed all at once.

soul The relationship between immersion and self-nullification is alluded to by the fact that the letters used to spell the word "to immerse" [*taval*] can be rearranged to spell the word "to nullify" [*batel* — "b" and "v" are interchangeable in this case].

A *Tzaddik* (righteous man) in *Kabbalah* is compared to a fish, which can never be torn from its source. The primordial state of the world was a Mikvah — a watery mass. 70% of the world is water, as is 70% of our bodies. Through Mikvah, G-d reminds us, "Return to your source. Come back to the water. Don't waste your life walking this earth, caught up with the world and self, ignorant of your source."

When a woman immerses in the heavenly waters of the Mikvah, she returns to her source of life. She leaves behind more than just her makeup and clothing. She sheds her ego and her sense of self. She is immersed in something transcendent, and at that moment she achieves purity and rises to a level at which she is able to become receptive to holiness.

Water is also symbolic of Torah, and when we immerse completely in the "waters of waters," we soften our heart and give strength to the G-dly soul to combat the *Yetzer Hara* (evil inclination). The mikvah experience strengthens our ability to channel our natural tendencies in the most productive and meaningful way possible. We achieve a personal and spiritual victory of the G-dly soul over the natural tendencies.

mind The moment of entry to the Mikvah is a double embrace for a woman with G-d: physical and spiritual at once.

When we immerse our whole body, we express our recognition that everything comes from G-d. This personal and intimate time with G-d aligns our perspective, opening up a unique ability for direct and laser-focused awareness of G-d in every moment of our lives.

Immersion transforms all that lurks in one's inner "murky waters," a little bit at a time. This brings one to an elevated spiritual state which helps prepare for the *mitzvah* that follows, a union that is permeated with holiness through the Mikvah experience.

Reflect:

- While immersing in these heavenly waters, envision yourself submerging in your source of life. Envision G-d's protective and loving embrace. Envision yourself becoming totally one with G-d. Allow yourself to let go with trust in your Creator. Envision G-d's holy light flowing through your entire being.

- Envision your soul, a part of G-d, shining bright. Thank G-d for your soul that gives you life each day. Through these heavenly waters, your soul becomes one again with the other half of your G-dly soul, your beloved husband. L'chaim!

Tapping Into Your Potential

A step-by-step process to reveal your soul through Mikvah:

Section 1: This is the area of the ritual bath where the woman actually immerses.

Section 2: This area (which is below the actual Mikvah) is a gathering pool where rainwater is stored. In Hebrew it is called a *bor*. The rainwater validates the tap water, making it kosher for ritual immersion.

Section 3: Two openings allow the rainwater to merge with the tap water. This symbolism describes the relationship between body and soul, an experience that takes place at the time of Mikvah immersion.

The two openings can be seen as love and fear of *Hashem* that bring in the holy rainwater and transform the regular water into a kosher Mikvah. So, too, love and fear of *Hashem* flowing into our thoughts, speech and actions transform them into holy endeavors.

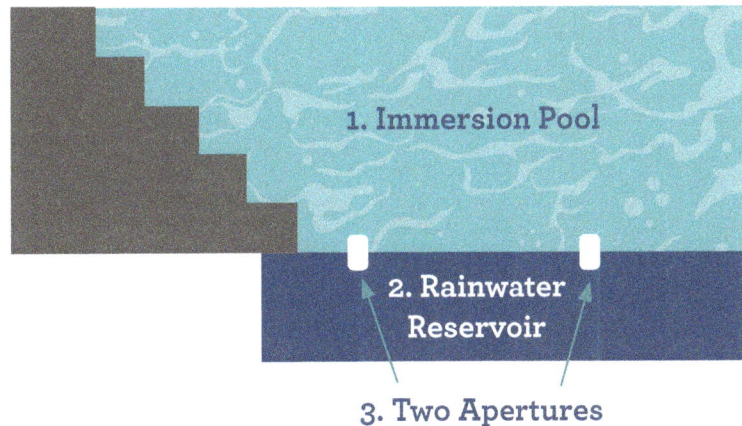

1. Immersion Pool

2. Rainwater Reservoir

3. Two Apertures

A Meditation for Immersion

Begin with your breathing. Concentrate on the thought that breath is the life force of the body. Every time you take a breath, a *neshima*, you connect your soul, your *Neshama*, to your body.

Take deep, regular breaths until you are breathing in a steady rhythm. With each inhalation, visualize that you are breathing in everything that is good: tranquility, love, harmony, and optimism. With each exhalation, breathe out everything that is troublesome: tension, sadness, bitterness, anger, and pessimism.

Picture yourself peacefully preparing for the Mikvah with genuine contentment and joy.

You are stress-free. You are worry-free.

As you visualize yourself preparing, remember that you possess the power to keep your love ever-growing and blossoming. All of your efforts are planting seeds of love and unity between you and your husband. This love shines in you and overflows into all of your relationships. Your love creates peace in the entire world.

Just like you bathe in warm water, you have the power to soften your heart by soaking in a bath of Torah. When you internalize the teachings of *Chassidus*, your animal soul is purified. Torah learning elevates your thoughts, speech, and actions – transforming the animal soul with the holiness of G-d's wisdom.

Focus on your G-dly soul and concentrate on uniting with G-d by merging your emotions with your Torah learning. Verbalize the following statement: "I know that Torah and *tefillot* (prayers) are the most effective way to strengthen myself against the evil inclination."

You make sure that no foreign substances intervene between you and the Mikvah waters. As you examine yourself, tell yourself, "I am cleansing my heart of past hurts and wounded feelings. I will not hold onto grudges. I forgive those who hurt me. The present is now. The present has infinite potential. I am letting go of the past and washing away negative emotions to bond with my spouse in true unity."

As you search the hard-to-reach places, remind yourself to work on refining the more subtle aspects of your being, like the tone of your voice. You smile in the mirror and resolve to add more loving smiles to your day. You are ready to do what it takes to bring joy and maintain a happy spirit in your life.

After you complete the preparations, you make sure not come into contact with any "sticky substances." Tell yourself, "I am free of any negative thoughts that might stick to me as I prepare for intimacy."

You see the pool of water, and you remember the meaning of the Mikvah structure. You are aware of your G-dly soul – pure and holy – as it trickles down into your animal soul. The two apertures of the Mikvah remind you to purify, not only your external but also your internal thoughts.

Beautiful Like A Bride Meditation

Get into a comfortably seated position on a chair that supports your head and arms as well as your back. Allow your feet to touch the ground. Feel grateful to G-d for your feet that will be holding you up in good stead, helping you go forward. Squeeze your toes tightly, until you feel the tension. After a count of three, relax your toes and release the tension there.

Feel grateful for your helping hands. Form them into fists until you feel the tension. Count to three. Then slowly open your hands and release the pressure.

Feel grateful for your face. Tighten your forehead, cheeks, and lips. Count to three and release the tension.

Thank G-d for your vision while you close your eyes. Tighten them and relax them. Express your thanks for your body that is the abode for your soul. Tense your back and shoulder muscles. Lift your shoulders. After counting to three, slowly let them drop as you release the tension.

You now feel completely relaxed. Feel lighter, as a soothing wave of relaxation flows over and through you. Your heart is beating calmly with a greater rapture, and your face is radiating with an ever-present smile. You feel sensual. Your eyes sparkle with that magical look of delight. You long for the other — your essence and beauty, bonding in perfect unity.

You are ready! You are calm yet elated. You are entirely immersed in the waters. You feel alive, vibrant and refreshed. You emerge anew and pure! Greater feelings of hope — *tikvah*, permeate you as you think of the word Mikvah. (Both words, *tikvah* and Mikvah, share the same Hebrew letters.) The past is a story already told, the future a story yet to unfold, but the present is a gift that is ours to behold. You have hope – and know, more than ever before, that you can have a loving relationship. You know that everything is possible. This moment is new. Transformation is happening.

You feel the purity of Mikvah influencing every aspect of your being and directing your every move. Even your small actions in the present have an incalculable impact on all future generations. Think of *Hashem* and fill yourself with hope. Realize that with G-d's help everything is possible; the seemingly bad will be transformed to good.

As you leave the heavenly holy waters, you are ready to take this experience with you into your daily life. With this in mind, verbalize the following statements: "I resolve, *bli neder* (without taking a vow), to adopt a positive action, emotion, or character trait to allow more joy and harmony into our marriage." Committing yourself to this course of action at this moment has unlimited potential for good.

You see the garments of a bride. You don your beautiful clothes, recalling the exuberance you felt when you were a bride. You long to rekindle your fiery love. Say to yourself: "I am prepared for the holy bond of intimacy." Your positive thoughts glow. Your words of kindness exalt you. Your good deeds keep the garments of your soul white, pure and beautiful.

You are ready to unite as ONE in mind, body and soul.

Blessing Recited During Mikvah Immersion

בָּרוּךְ אַתָּה ה' אֱלֹקֵינוּ מֶלֶךְ הָעוֹלָם
אֲשֶׁר קִדְּשָׁנוּ בְּמִצְוֹתָיו וְצִוָּנוּ עַל הַטְבִלָה

**Blessed are You G-d, our G-d, King of the universe,
Who sanctified us with Your commandments,
and commanded us concerning immersion.**

Mikvah is one of the three special and unique *mitzvot* specifically given to the Jewish woman. When performing any one of her three *mitzvot*, it is an opportune time for the woman to pray to G-d for whatever she would like. The gates of heaven are open at this time, and G-d awaits the prayers of the Jewish woman.

Envision your prayer being uplifted by holy angels and the doors being opened to reach the final place of G-d's glorious throne. And with sweet music all around, G-d is receiving your prayers. All the portals are opened because of your efforts to fulfill this *mitzvah* in the most beautiful way.

CHAPTER FOUR

HOLY INTIMACY

An Act that Mirrors G-d

*H*ashem, our Creator, allows us to take part in the very act of procreation. Of all possible activity, Jewish intimacy contains the highest potential for spirituality as a means through which the husband and wife express their holiness. At its highest peak, the intimate union in a Jewish marriage brings holiness beyond the home and into the world at large. This happens through the spiritual, emotional and physical bond between husband and wife.

"There is no greater accomplishment that man can achieve than to bond with his soulmate to procreate."

According to Jewish thought, a husband and wife originally begin as one soul before birth, split in half when the first of the two is conceived. Marriage, and more specifically intimacy between a husband and wife, represents the reunion of the halves as a single entity. In describing the reunion that marital intimacy represents, the Torah tells us, "Therefore shall a man leave his father and mother and cleave unto his wife, and they shall become one flesh." (Genesis 2:24)

Complete Oneness in Marriage

We learn that man was created from dust, and the woman from the rib of the man. A woman is a helpmate for her husband. In order to fulfill her mission as helpmate, she joins with him so that he may fulfill the *mitzvah* of *"P'ru U'revu"* — "Be fruitful and multiply."

G-d gives the woman the gift of making space for the other so she can become a vessel to receive her husband fully. When the husband is the *mashpiah* (giver) and the wife the *mekabel* (receiver), there is a balance so that *shalom bayit* endures.

One of the most important parts to marriage is intimacy, and the *ketubah* makes known to every Jewish couple that they are to engage in intimacy without feeling any guilt or shame for fulfilling G-d's will. It is His Will that created the Divine gift of intimacy. When we view intimacy as holy, we can feel trust and acceptance in our marriage.

Our Sages teach that nothing is more important than *shalom bayit*. We learn that G-d Himself said to *Moshe Rabbeinu*, "Erase My Name" in order to keep a husband and wife together. (Laws of *Sotah*).

Marital Relations

A wife begins to prepare for intimacy with the simple act of thinking about her husband in a positive light and focusing on how she can meet his needs. This can make a significant difference in a marriage.

On the night of a woman's immersion in the Mikvah, a tremendous spiritual power is available to her. In addition to being given the opportunity to connect with her husband on a physical level, she has the chance to connect with him emotionally and spiritually. As it is a time at which a new life may be formed, it is also an appropriate time for them both to connect to *Hashem*—their Partner in a child's creation. The proper performance of any *mitzvah* requires *kavanah*, the focused concentration of our mental and spiritual faculties. The *mitzvah* will be acceptable to *Hashem* no matter how perfunctorily it is performed, but its value both to G-d and to ourselves increases exponentially in relation to our level of *kavanah*. As is true with most human endeavors, the reward is commensurate with the effort.

This applies equally—Rabbi Yitzchak Ginsburgh says especially—to the realm of marital relations. Many sources state that the purity of the parents' thoughts and behavior during marital relations determines the nature of their offspring. According to the *Zohar* (3:81a), the most propitious time for marital relations is after midnight, not only for reasons of modesty but because at that time the gates of heaven are fully open, and a couple can elicit a soul of a higher order.

During marital relations, a couple should try to keep in mind the following intentions:

1. To provide one's spouse with pleasure and fulfillment. The Torah considers a man's obligation to "gladden his wife" (Deut. 24:5) so basic to a happy marriage that a newly-married man is exempted from military service for the entire first year of marriage so that he may stay home and keep his wife company. "Gladdening" also refers to affectionate words a man should speak to his wife before relations. When the couple gives each other pleasure and delight, G-d experiences a tremendous delight through their holy intimacy.

2. To fulfill the *mitzvah* to "be fruitful and multiply" (Genesis 1:28), which includes, on a deeper level, the desire to bring G-d-fearing, holy souls into the world. This *kavanah* is applicable even for a physically infertile couple, because marital relations carried out in a holy manner create spiritual "offspring" (e.g., thoughts of repentance that influence other Jews to return to a Torah life, or souls of future converts).

3. To recognize that G-d is Omnipresent, and to attempt to emulate in the marital union the Divine union of G-d and the *Shechinah* (the soul

of all the Jewish people). This is the highest level of *kavanah,* for if a couple has this intention in mind, their successful and loving union will be replicated in the reconciliation and reuniting, so to speak, of G-d and His people.

The ultimate culmination of all these intentions, Rabbi Ginsburgh explains, is that through a holy marital union a couple can give life to holy souls, every one of which adds to the world its consciousness of G-d, until "the earth will be full of the knowledge of G-d as the water covers the seabed." This knowledge will serve to unite all of mankind, Jews and non-Jews alike, and hasten the coming of the *Moshiach.*

Holy Relations that don't result in a child being born, still create holy souls in higher realms and positive spiritual energy. The positive energy is felt in the couple's personal relationships, in the atmosphere of their home, and in their relationship with others. The positive effects go beyond their immediate surroundings.

Sefer Pischei Chaim offers a selection of Torah verses for spouses to recite before marital relations and contemplate afterward:

In the beginning G-d created the heaven and the earth. (Genesis 1:1);

And the children of Israel were fruitful, and increased abundantly, and multiplied, and grew exceedingly mighty; and the land was filled with them. (Exodus 1:7);

Speak unto all the congregation of the children of Israel, and say to them: You shall be holy; for I the Lord your G-d am holy. (Leviticus 19:2);

May the Lord bless you and protect you; May the Lord shine His face upon you, and be gracious to you; May the Lord uplift His face to you and give you peace. (Numbers 6:24-26);

May the Lord, the G-d of your forefathers, increase you a thousand-fold, and bless you, as He has promised you! (Deuteronomy 1:11);

The Torah that Moses commanded us is a heritage [for] the congregation of Jacob. (Deut. 33:4);

And in all [carried out with the] strong hand, and in all the great terror, which Moses wrought in the sight of all Israel. (Deut. 34:12);

And he shall be like a tree planted by streams of water, that brings forth its fruit in its season, and whose leaf does not wither; and in whatever he does he shall prosper. (Psalms 1:3).

It is also suggested that on the day of a woman's immersion, she and her husband donate extra charity as a merit for the new soul.

A Delicate Question

Q: How does one handle a situation where a husband is mistaken about a Halachic question that pertains to their marital union?

A wife should try to avoid telling her husband that he is wrong morally. This cannot be reiterated enough. For we learn from our Sages that at all costs, even a rabbi should not embarrass a husband in front of his wife by saying that what he is doing is wrong. If the rabbi responds to a question the couple has posed, he is careful about fostering *shalom bayit* between them. No *mitzvah* is more important than another *mitzvah*, yet *shalom bayit* reigns supreme.

The rabbi knows that, regardless of the situation the couple is grappling with, it is a huge priority for him to protect the sanctity of their marriage and their *shalom bayit*. Thus he will not make any direct remark to the couple that would cause the wife to lose respect for her husband. Even if something the husband is doing is not 100% kosher, the rabbi will say, "Give me some time to think about the answer to your question. It is no simple matter; I have to check as there are differing opinions."

He does this so that he can then speak with the husband privately. If he were to correct the husband there on the spot, the wife's respect for her husband would decrease. And at the very moment the wife feels a lack of respect for her husband, she begins to lose a little of her own personal honor. Why is this? As we know, a husband and wife become one underneath the *chuppah*. Therefore when the husband loses his honor, she loses her honor as well, especially since she so desires to honor and respect her husband. This is why no rabbi will try to interfere publicly in front of both a husband and a wife.

Rabbis who have experience and success in helping couples know that it is more beneficial to the *shalom bayit* when the rabbi makes a correction privately with the husband so as not to make the husband look unknowledgeable in front of his wife. How important it is for the wife to remember that, even if she is technically right about a certain *halacha*, her husband was born from dust, and he needs her to be his helper, not a "mother figure" or a "policewoman." If she were to act as his rabbi, that surely would diminish the peace in the home and even cause strife in the marriage.

A Meditation for Mikvah Night

Begin with your breathing. Concentrate on the thought that breath is the life force of the body and that every time you take a breath, a *neshima*, you connect your soul, your *Neshama*, to your body.

Take deep, regular breaths until you are breathing in a steady rhythm. With each inhalation, visualize that you are breathing in everything that is good: tranquility, love, harmony, and optimism. With each exhalation, breathe out everything that is troublesome: tension, sadness, bitterness, anger, and pessimism.

Now, visualize the holy cloud that graced our first Mother Sarah's tent. Sarah's tent was sacred just like the Temple itself, and Rivkah echoed her in every way. Your holy Mitzvah of immersing in the Mikvah has recreated the cloud of glory for you. You are following in the footsteps of our Matriarchs, Sarah and Rivkah. Miracles are unfolding in your life.

Envision the Divine cloud that accompanied our people for 40 years in the hot desert and the cloud that rested on the *Mishkan* (tabernacle), the portable desert sanctuary. Visualize your own white protective cloud of G-d coming closer and closer to you. Its presence is calming. The cloud stops before you, hovering like a magic carpet. It is surrounding you on all four sides. It is a Divine embrace. Take a leap and step onto the cloud. It rises, higher and higher, lifting you above the obstacles in your path. All your worries melt away. You trust and have complete faith in G-d. You feel safe and serene and as light as the cloud itself.

Take a deep breath and recite a prayer to G-d. "Please provide my family and me with our needs in the physical realm to facilitate greater accomplishments in the spiritual realm. Bless our efforts to shine your light. Bless each member of our family with health and happiness. Give me the strength to apply the wisdom and holiness I have attained so that my dream of love and peace will be fulfilled."

You feel the cloud rising higher than you ever dreamed possible and closer to *Hashem*. Your soul feels free, and your heart overflows with love for G-d and your soulmate. Your feet are dancing and rising higher and higher until you see *Hashem*'s light surrounding you. You savor the peaceful colors and beauty, the caressing warmth of the sun shining above. You feel at ease.

The cloud of glory brings you to the entrance of your sanctuary. You step off into the most beautiful and holy surroundings you can imagine. As your feet touch the ground, all the barriers to trust and love between you and your spouse disappear. Your heart is calm. You feel joyful and you smile. You feel beautiful. Your eyes sparkle with a magical look of delight. You see the smile on the face of your husband.

Visualize a flame. It is your passionate love flickering in your soul and flowing out to your husband. Your intimate bond is sacred and holy. Your holy of holies, your bedroom, is a haven of love and joy. It is a place to unwind, where you connect to your true selves. Here your essence and beauty unite with your soulmate's essence and beauty to create an infinite bond of perfect unity. Your soul sings. Your soul is complete.

CHAPTER FIVE

MIKVAH STORIES

We can approach the Divine in a way like never before when we understand the deeper meaning of Mikvah.

Opportunity Knocks

by Miriam Yerushalmi

If only we realized just how close to Divinity we are when we immerse, we would be so much more eager to grasp this extraordinary opportunity to beseech *Hashem* with our prayers.

A story from the *Frierdiker Rebbe* illustrates the magnitude of this *mitzvah*. Once, a great Torah scholar asked the famous Chassidic master Rabbi Meir of Premishlan for help on a passage in the *Rambam*. Rabbi Meir arranged to see him the next day. Together they studied the *Rambam*, which proved an enlightening experience. When asked how he was able to figure out the difficulty in the passage, Rabbi Meir replied, "When Meir goes to the Mikvah, he passes through heaven, and he asked to be led through the *heichal* (courtyard) of the *Rambam*, who taught me this subject."

If we could only keep this story in mind while we immerse we would be filled with gratitude at the thought that *Hashem* has entrusted us with this *mitzvah*. Now we can experience Mikvah night like never before.

Angels

Excerpted from Bread, Fire and Water *by Auriel Silbiger*

The Mikvah lady calls out the word 'kosher.'

"'Kosher'?"

"Yes, kosher. And do you know what happens then?"

"What?" I wasn't sure whether to be nervous.

"The angels hear the pronouncement, and they swoop down and grab that word as it floats past them, and lift it, carrying it up, up, throughout the heavens, through each of the heavenly realms. All the while they are rising, they are echoing the word 'kosher,' singing in unison. All of the heavenly beings hear the word 'kosher' and echo it, too. They join the other angels and seraphim, flying up and up until they reach the Heavenly Throne itself. There, they bring this word before G-d. In that moment, G-d Himself pronounces your immersion kosher. That is why it is in that split second that one has the opportunity to tell or ask G-d whatever it is that one wants."

Talk about an open portal! I take it back! I haven't lost the faculty of prayer, for the steps that we take to prepare for and use the Mikvah are a sure form of prayer. Why, for all the tears shed in prayer by all the women at the Mikvah, it is astonishing that only the ocean waters are salty.

The Mikvah lady reflects:

My client recites the blessing. She wants me to say the words with her. I can say the words with her if she is unsure of the Hebrew, but I can never take away, or even fully share this moment with her. It wholly, totally and independently, belongs to her. I watch carefully as she immerses a second time.

I can barely articulate the word "kosher" as in a sudden flash of insight it becomes clear to me that the angels who take the word "kosher" before G-d have a particularly easy job because they do not fly heavenward alone. They are ably aided by all of the Mikvah users and Mikvah attendants from throughout our history. All those Jewish women who used the Mikvah, many of them under the most harrowing of circumstances, each with at least as many good reasons as we have today not to uphold this extraordinary observance. They all unite now to carry word of yet another immersion upward.

There is a roaring in my ears as loud as the ocean as she immerses for the third and final time.

"Kosher."

Yes, kosher. The physical act of sanctifying time, space and ourselves. An act that is simply right. I am convinced for now, beyond any doubt, that there is something about all of this that will remain "kosher"– fit and right – forever.

She emerges from the water. Each of us feels renewed and refreshed. Each of us is equipped to go back into the world and start the rest of our lives again.

A Ten Year Wait for Children

By Miriam Yerushalmi

After one of my classes on Mikvah, a woman approached me and asked if she could speak to me privately. She seemed very sad, and after we spoke I understood why. She and her husband had been married for almost 10 years, but they had no children yet. She told me that she did go to the Mikvah, but it was an emotionally difficult process for her that she did unenthusiastically by rote, trying to get through it as quickly as possible.

I shared with her some of the Rebbe's letters on the topic in which he recommended that the *mitzvah* be done *"bedi'uk,"* very carefully and conscientiously. I also suggested that she take classes to learn more about how to perform this *mitzvah* properly according to the law.

The woman accepted these recommendations and took them to heart. She hadn't realized that she missed out on some of the details involved in the laws of Mikvah. The next time that she went to Mikvah, she performed the miztvah *"bediuk"*—with careful attention to the detail of the law—and she became pregnant.

The Mikvah Transformation

By Miriam Yerushalmi

I'd like to share another amazing story involving one of my clients and Mikvah.

I'll never forget a client whom I met during one of my trips back to Israel. Because of major delays at the airport, I arrived at my home only minutes before candle lighting on the eve of Rosh Hashanah. On the second day of Rosh Hashanah, the children and I joined my husband on the street as he blew *shofar* for those who had been unable to attend synagogue. One of the people who came to hear him blow *shofar* was an acquaintance of mine whom I hadn't seen in more than three years. She told me that she must see me that very night. As I hadn't yet settled in after my travels, I replied that I would be happy to see her the next morning. But she insisted that it was critical that we meet as soon as possible, so I relented.

When we met late that night, she told me that a friend of hers was in a state of crisis. "She began having panic attacks about a year ago. She's been seeing therapists and psychiatrists who have prescribed all kinds of medications, but nothing's helped." The woman was feeling acutely depressed. My friend begged me to see her that night and, despite my jet lag, I agreed.

When I met the woman, I assumed that she wasn't religiously observant, as she was wearing slacks and her hair was uncovered, although she was married. I hesitated to speak freely because I was afraid that if she thought I was shoving religion down her throat or taking too mystical an approach to her very down-to-

earth problem, she would dismiss my advice out-of-hand.

Suddenly I decided to be direct, and I began to tell her about the concept of bringing healing by making oneself a greater vessel for spirituality. I chose Mikvah observance as the example by which to explain this concept. As soon as the words came out of my mouth, though, I regretted the choice, thinking it would have no relevance to her. But before I could stop and offer another example, she stared at me in shock and said, "I can't believe you said that."

Taken aback, I waited for her to explain. She was so emotional that it was hard for her to speak. "Tell me," I insisted gently.

She took a deep breath and began. "I used to go to the Mikvah until about a year ago. Then I began to have irregular bleeding, and I had to go so often that I got frustrated and stopped going altogether."

Amazed, I asked her when her panic attacks had begun.

She stood there, almost frozen, and said, "My goodness, just about the time I stopped going to the Mikvah."

I blessed her that she should immediately make a decision to return to her previous commitment and, moreover, go to a Mikvah teacher in order to review the precise *halachic* requirements for preparing for immersion. Then and there she committed herself to doing so.

That night when she returned home, her panic attacks evaporated, along with

her depression. She phoned me later to share the good news and said that her children—who had not seen her smile for almost a year—were delighted to see their mother back to herself.

The following week, at her request, I accompanied her to her place of work and I saw with my own eyes her co-workers' amazement at her transformation.

Had I not witnessed this story myself, I would not have believed it. But I did witness it—and many other similar miracles. When a disorder results from spiritual factors, those factors must be addressed. Although making yourself an adequate vessel for the light of holiness may seem tangential and even irrelevant to the problems you are facing, it may actually be the most powerful factor affecting the situation.

Note: At times medication may be necessary to stabilize an emotional or psychiatric imbalance, especially if there is any danger to oneself or others. At other times medication is given in order to help a person become focused and receptive to getting necessary treatment and information. In such cases, I do not hesitate to refer clients to the appropriate professionals. To do otherwise would be dangerously naïve as well as unethical.

A Special Wish

Excerpted from Thank You G-d for Making Me a Woman *by Rabbi Aaron Raskin*

A congregant once told me about his grandparents who arrived in Bismarck, North Dakota in 1905, a place that attracted many German immigrants. They had four daughters, all of whom had little interest in Judaism. One daughter, Beatrice, even became an atheist as a defense mechanism to avoid getting caught up in politics because of her religion. After some time, the family moved to Minnesota where Beatrice married and gave birth to a daughter. Her daughter Esther encountered Chabad in Minnesota, and eventually attended the Bais Chana School for girls where she met Rabbi Manis Friedman, who became her teacher and mentor. With time, Esther became religious and ended up marrying a follower of Chabad teachings. Esther was married for a number of years but was unfortunately unable to bear any children. She went to the Mikvah monthly as she was supposed to, and studied the laws carefully to make sure she did everything right. She even went to doctors and tried in vitro fertilization and other such procedures to no avail.

Finally, she wrote a letter to the Lubavitcher Rebbe about her situation and asked for a blessing. A few days later she received a telephone call from Rabbi Laibel Groner, one of the Rebbe's secretaries. "The Rebbe suggested that you ask your mother to go to the Mikvah." Esther asked Beatrice if she would be willing to go, but being as she was an atheist, she refused. Esther wrote back to the Rebbe telling of her mother's refusal and soon received another phone call from

Rabbi Groner. "The Rebbe suggests that you ask your grandmother to go to the Mikvah." Esther called up her grandmother and asked her if she would be willing to go to the Mikvah so she would be blessed with a child.

Esther's grandmother asked her husband what he thought of the prospect and his response was immediate, "What wouldn't a grandparent do for a grandchild? Of course, you should go."

The grandmother went to the Mikvah, and a month later Esther became pregnant with the first of her nine children.

This story clearly shows that the *mitzvah* of Mikvah is not only a personal *mitzvah* but also one that affects your children for generations to come. It also proves that it is never too late to start, and even if you're at a point where you only need to go once, retroactively you can still impact many generations to come.

The Rebbe's Advice

Excerpted from Thank You G-d for Making Me a Woman *by Rabbi Aaron Raskin*

A woman once wrote a letter to the Rebbe, in which she expressed how upset she was that her Jewish son was living with a non-Jewish woman. Theologically and philosophically, marriage between a Jew and non-Jew is not allowed and could be very counterproductive for both sides. The Rebbe asked if the child was born in purity, and if not, it was not too late for the mother to rectify this and immerse in a Mikvah.

How can someone make things "right"?

Luckily, Mikvah is a *mitzvah* that can retroactively repair the damage, because the spiritual world is not bound by time or space.

1. Start going to Mikvah now.

2. Try to influence at least two other women to go to Mikvah as well.

3. Increase in giving charity, not necessarily by giving large amounts, but rather in the frequency to giving. Keep a charity box in your kitchen and put a few coins in every day. Maimonides teaches that a *mitzvah* is performed each time you put a coin into a charity box, so the more times you give the more *mitzvot* you do. This *mitzvah* is significant because charity brings atonement and redemption, so it is a fitting action to perform before going into the Mikvah.

A Mother's Mitzvah Helps Her Daughter

Excerpted from Thank You G-d for Making Me a Woman *by Rabbi Aaron Raskin*

According to Jewish law the Mikvah needs to contain a quantity of forty *se'ah*, a Talmudic measurement equal to about 160-200 gallons of water. The number forty represents transformation. For example, the flood that G-d brought upon the world during the time of Noah lasted forty days and nights in order to purify the world like a Mikvah.

The *mitzvah* of Mikvah is not only relevant for younger women, who are capable of having children and still menstruate, but also for women who have reached or passed menopause. If a woman did not go to the Mikvah after her last period, she can — and is encouraged to — immerse in the Mikvah one last time, as long as she is still married. Not only will she now be in a permanent state of holiness and purity, but going to the Mikvah with the proper intent could retroactively fix all the immersion times she had missed out on until now.

A young girl was suffering from severe emotional issues, so her mother wrote a letter to the Rebbe requesting a blessing for her emotional health. The Rebbe asked his secretaries to find out whether or not the mother kept the laws of Mikvah and if the daughter was born in purity. The Rebbe's question implied that this could be the reason for her instability, and that the mother could retroactively correct it by going to the Mikvah.

The Power of One

There is a true story that happened in a *yechidus* (private audience) between Rabbi Gutnick from Australia and the Lubavitcher Rebbe. The Rebbe asked this rabbi to start a *Taharat Hamishpacha* (Family Purity) class in his *shul*. Rabbi Gutnick answered that he knew his congregants: they were very interested in *Kabbalah* and mysticism, but not in Family Purity.

"Try anyway," said the Rebbe. So the rabbi, a true *Chassid*, implemented the Rebbe's directive. He paid for advertisements and hired a secretary to phone the congregants. Week after week they phoned, but in the end only one student came to the class. When the rabbi returned to report to the Rebbe, he mentioned sadly that only one student showed up after all the time and money that had been invested.

The Rebbe brilliantly answered, "How many mothers did *Moshe Rabbeinu* have?"

CHAPTER SIX

LETTERS FROM THE REBBE

By the Grace of G-d
14th of Sivan, 5724
Brooklyn, NY

Mrs. —- Albany, N.Y.

Blessings and Greetings:

I am in receipt of your letter of May 21st, in which you write about your background and some highlights of your life. In reply, I will address myself at once to the essential point in your letter, namely your attitude towards religious observance, as you describe in your letter, and especially toward the particular *mitzvah* which is essential for a happy married life, namely *Taharas Hamishpacha*. You write that you do not understand the importance of the *mitzvah*, etc. This is not surprising, as is clear from the analogy of a small child's being unable to understand a professor who is advanced in knowledge. Bear in mind that the dissimilarity between the small child and the advanced professor is only a difference in degree and not in kind, inasmuch as the child may, in due course, not only attain the same level as the professor, but even surpass him. It is quite otherwise regarding the difference between a created being, be he the wisest person on earth, and the Creator Himself. How can we, humans, expect to understand the infinite wisdom of the Creator? It is only because of G-d's great kindness that He has revealed certain reasons with regard to certain *mitzvot* so that we can get some sort of glimpse or insight into them. It is quite clear that G-d has given us the various commandments for our own sake and not in order

Taharas Hamishpacha has a direct bearing not only on the mutual happiness of the husband and wife, but also on the well-being and happiness of their offspring, their children and children's children.

to benefit Him. It is therefore clear what the sensible attitude towards the *mitzvot* should be. If this is so with regard to any *mitzvah*, how much more is it so with regard to the said *mitzvah* of *Taharas Hamishpacha*, which has a direct bearing not only on the mutual happiness of the husband and wife, but also on the well-being and happiness of their offspring, their children and children's children. It is equally clear that parents are always anxious to do everything possible for their children, even if there is only a very small chance that their efforts would materialize, and even if these efforts entail great difficulties. How much more so is it true in this case where the benefit to be derived is very great and lasting, while the sacrifice is negligible by comparison. Even where the difficulties are not entirely imaginary, it is certain that they become less and less challenging with actual observance of the *mitzvah*, so they eventually disappear altogether.

Needless to say, I am aware of the "argument" that there are many non-observant married couples who are seemingly happy, and so forth. The answer is simple. First of all, it is well- known that G-d is very merciful and patient, and He waits for the erring sinner to return to Him in sincere repentance. Secondly, appearances are deceptive, and one can never know what the true facts are about somebody else's life, especially as certain things relating to children and other personal matters are, for obvious reasons, kept in strict confidence.

As a matter of fact, in regard to the observance of *Taharas Hamishpacha*, even the plain statistics of reports and tables by specialists, doctors and sociologists etc., who cannot be considered partial towards the religious Jew, clearly show the benefits which accrued to those Jewish circles which observed *Taharas Hamishpacha*. These statistics have also been disseminated in various publications, but it is not my intention to dwell on this at length in this letter.

My intention in writing all the above is, of course, not to admonish or preach, but in the hope that upon the receipt of my letter, you will consider the matter more deeply, and that you will at once begin to observe the *mitzvah* of *Taharas Hamishpacha*, within the framework of the general Jewish way of life, which our Creator has clearly given to given to us in His Torah, which is called *Toras Chaim*, the Law of Life. Even if it seems to you that you have some difficulties to overcome, you may be certain that you will overcome them, and that the difficulties are only in the initial stages.

I understand that in your community there are young couples who are observant, and you could discuss this matter with them and find out all the laws and regulations of *Taharas Hamishpacha*.

If, however, you find it inconvenient to seek the knowledge from friends, there are booklets which have been published which contain the desired information, including a list of places where a Mikvah is available...Moreover, inasmuch as the *mitzvot* are also the channels through which to receive G-d's blessings, it is not surprising that a lack of observance prevents the fulfillment of G-d's blessings.

(Signature)

By the Grace of G-d
7th Menachem Av, 5740
Brooklyn, NY

Greetings and Blessings:

I received your letter and *Pidyon*, and I will remember you in prayer when I visit the holy resting place of my father-in-law of saintly memory, for the fulfillment of your heart's desires for the good, especially to bring up your children to a life of Torah, *Chuppah* and Good Deeds, in good health physically and spiritually. Although what follows is self-evident, its importance requires its being emphasized, at any rate briefly.

To begin with, it is obvious that the said blessing of healthy offspring both physically and spiritually is largely dependent on the conduct of the parents. For just as the physical health and constitution of the parents have an impact on the physical health of the children, so it is also the case mentally and spiritually.

Indeed, as every intelligent person understands, the spiritual aspect is stronger than the body, so that the order should be reversed: namely, the spiritual impact is predominant. Torah, *Toras Emes*, has declared that Jews are "believers the sons of believers," meaning that in addition to one's own belief in G-d, one has the cumulative heritage of countless generations, beginning with our father Abraham, the first believer, that the source of all blessings is G-d, the Creator

It is obvious that the said blessing of healthy offspring both physically and spiritually is largely dependent on the conduct of the parents.

and Master of the Universe. If a human being who introduces a certain system must give guidelines as to how the system works, how much more so it is to be expected that G-d would provide guidelines as to how a human being, and especially a Jew, must live. These guidelines were revealed at Sinai with the Giving of the Torah and *mitzvot*, which were transmitted from generation to generation, not only in content, but also in exact terms. Thus, the Torah provides the guidelines as to how Jews have to conduct their life, especially their family life. But inasmuch as a human being, however perfect he may be, is liable to fail occasionally, G-d has provided the way in which it can be rectified, namely by way of *teshuva* which, as our sages declare, was created even before the world. And *teshuva* is effective not only in respect to the future, but also retroactively to a large extent, inasmuch as G-d is omnipotent and is not restricted in any way. It is a matter of common experience that it is part of human nature that parents will make every sacrifice for the benefit of the children, even in a case where the benefit may not be certain, but has prospects. All the above is by way of introduction to my earnest plea that regardless of how it was in the past, you will strengthen your commitment and adherence to the will of G-d, the Creator of all blessings, particularly in the area of the strict fulfillment of the laws and regulations of *Taharas Hamishpacha* which, aside from the essential aspect of their being Divine imperatives, have the Divine promise of reward in terms of healthy offspring, physically, mentally and spiritually.

Needless to say, when it comes to carrying out the commandments of G-d, it is absolutely irrelevant what neighbors or friends might say when they see a radical change in the everyday life. Herein is also the answer to many questions, including the question of why this or that *mitzvah* has to be observed. For a human being to question G-d's reasons for His *mitzvot* is actually contradictory to common sense. If one accepts them as Divine commandments, it would be presumptuous, indeed ridiculous, to equate, *lehavdil*, G-d's intellect to that of a human being.

By way of simple illustration, which I had occasion to use before: one would not expect an infant to understand the importance of nutrition as set forth by a professor who has dedicated his life to this subject, even though the difference between the infant and professor is only relative in terms of age and education, and in fact, the infant might some day even surpass the professor. There can be no such comparison between a created human being and the Creator, where the difference is absolute.

Needless to say, when it comes to carrying out the commandments of G-d, it is absolutely irrelevant what neighbors or friends might say when they see a radical change in the everyday life.

It should, therefore, be a matter of common sense to understand what the Torah, *Toras Emes*, explains clearly: that whatever doubts and difficulties a Jew may have in matters of Torah and *mitzvot* are only test of his faith in G-d, and that a person is equipped with the capacity to overcome such tests and distractions, for it would be illogical to assume that G-d would impose obligations which are beyond human capacity to fulfill. Indeed, if one has more difficult tests, it only proves that he has greater capacities to overcome them. In summary, just as when we received the Torah and *mitzvot* at Sinai, we accepted them on the basis of *naaseh* first and then *v'nishma*, namely on the basis of unconditional obedience and readiness to fulfill G-d's commandments regardless of our understanding of them rationally, so has our commitment been ever since. And while we must learn and try to understand as much as possible, prior knowledge and understanding must never be a condition for living up to the guidelines which G-d has given in regard to our actual way of life and conduct.

With blessing,

(Signature)

By the Grace of G-d
16th of Adar I, 5725
Brooklyn, NY

Blessings and Greetings:

I was pleased to receive your letter of the 15th of *Shevat*, in which you write about the successful initial meeting on *Taharas Hamishpacha*, and the fruitful beginnings.

It is, of course, unnecessary to emphasize to you the paramount importance of this cause. Nor do I think that it would require a great deal of persuasion to convince the other participants in the meeting of the vital importance of T*aharas Hamishpacha.*

Suffice it to say that even where a person may not be so meticulous insofar as he or she is concerned, there is no limit to the love and devotion of parents to their children, and their readiness to spare no sacrifice for their benefit.

Even if the observance of the laws and regulations of *Taharas Hamishpacha* entailed a certain effort or even sacrifice on the parents' part, surely it would be done eagerly, knowing that in addition to the essential thing of the need of observing G-d's commands for their own sake, these observances have a direct influence on children, and through them on grandchildren and so on.

Of what account, therefore, is a temporary inconvenience or effort by comparison to the everlasting benefits in terms of good health, physical and spiritual, and true Nachas, etc.

Of what account, therefore, is a temporary inconvenience or effort by comparison to the everlasting benefits in terms of good health, physical and spiritual, and true *Nachas*, etc. This is all the more true since the inconvenience or effort is smaller than imagined.

May G-d grant that this vital activity of *Taharas Hamishpacha* in your community should grow and expand, bringing even more members and participants, and may the observance of this essential law and regulation also stimulate the general observance of the Torah and *mitzvot*, where there is always room for improvement.

With blessing,

(Signature)

APPENDIX

Helping Women with OCD

Obsessive Compulsive Disorder (OCD) is a disorder of the mind. The sufferer is plagued with unwanted repetitive thoughts, ideas, images or impulses that run through the sufferer's mind like a film loop, over and over again. The person is led to compulsive behaviors that are repeated continuously in his or her attempt to get rid of the obsessive thoughts. Most people with OCD know that the behaviors do not make sense, but they cannot stop themselves from repeating them. Of course, OCD patients do not want these thoughts or behaviors to control them, and they find them disturbing. For some, the thoughts occur only once in a while and are mildly annoying. For others, the thoughts are constant. The behaviors tend to make them nervous and afraid of their lack of control.

There are many common OCD thoughts. One is fear of germs: these patients can be found repeatedly washing their hands. Through repetitive washing, they find temporary relief from the anxiety of contact with germs, but soon afterward the nervousness returns and they find themselves back once again at the sink, in yet another attempt to find some relief. There are also typical OCD behaviors that involve religious rituals. For example, a homemaker might obsess about milk touching meat products or dishes. On *Pesach*, one might fear that all *chametz* (leaven) has not been thoroughly removed. There is fear of *tumah* (impurity) in the *negel vasser* (hand-washing) basin, so the individual will wash and rewash.

Then there is the Mikvah OCD patient. Many *frum* (observant) women may not know they have this disorder. Because of their lack of awareness, these women have no clue that what they are suffering is a medically classified DSM (Diagnostic and Statistical Manual) disorder. Most of the time they usually function; however, in the area of ritual (and for some, in more than one area), their brains go haywire. OCD is what this author's Psych 101 professor called a broken-pocketed brain syndrome — meaning all other parts of the brain seem to work, except for this one part.

While to an outsider a woman preparing herself for the Mikvah might be praised for being extra-scrupulous, the OCD patient is operating in a different orbit. The scenario goes like this: First, the woman (call her Malkie) spends 10-15 minutes, twice a day, checking her *bedika* (white) cloths. She keeps asking herself, "Did I cover all areas? Are the *bedika* cloths completely white? Can I start counting? Did I check in the correct lighting?" During the few days before immersion, she begins the process. She then has the nagging thought that she did not sufficiently clean a particular part of her body. So she then cleans herself over and over again until she has scrubbed herself raw. Malkie checks the next area, her teeth. For over a half hour she continues flossing until her gums start to bleed. She cuts her nails all the way below the nail line until her fingers hurt, and then she removes the cuticles until they start to bleed as well. The preparation process is a living hell for these women. The agony they go through is unimaginable. Dinner is not cooked, laundry not folded — the to-do list never becomes marked off as "done" — because all Malkie has been doing the whole day is getting ready for the Mikvah.

The minute the Mikvah opens up, she is there, and she is the last to leave — way past the time the Mikvah was supposed to close. The hour is midnight. While in the Mikvah, she is super-stressed, since other women are waiting and the Mikvah lady is even knocking on her door to see if everything is okay. Alone and embarrassed, Malkie is on the verge of tears and questions herself, "What's wrong with me? Why am I not managing like other women?" She cries from deep within. "Help! Help! I need to finish and get going!" When she is finally done and ready to immerse, she breaks out in a cold sweat and wonders, "Did I do the proper *bedika*? Did I check enough, and scrub enough?" Even her red, raw skin does not convince her she did it right. She immerses with doubts and concerns and feels terrible that she has inadvertently caused the Mikvah attendant to stay late, while her husband has to wait and wait again. Coming home, she is embarrassed once again. She does not reveal the problem to her husband and keeps her secret deep inside.

Her obsessive thoughts creep up again, making her feel too non-kosher to be intimate with him. She panics and wants to call the *Rav* again. Yes, again. So she phones the *Rav*, who reassures her that after the fact, even if she did not scrub an area of her thigh, she is still kosher. She explains several times, and the Rav reassures her again and again. As Malkie hangs up the phone, she broods, "Did I explain myself clearly to the *Rav*? Did I give him all the details?" Now it is 1 AM, and she is exhausted. She gives in and has relations. Her husband at this point may think, "What is wrong? Is this what every man goes through with his wife? Is this what G-d has intended"? No one has ever prepared him for this!

Unfortunately, the turmoil has just begun. Now Malkie wonders if she has caused her husband to sin by having relations with her when she may be impure. If she has conceived, she wonders whether the new baby will be "kosher." Every day she worries; every day she panics. She wants to get pregnant, but then again she hopes she does not, because of her fear of having created an "impure" baby. Then the day comes, and she finds out she is pregnant. She has mixed feelings, mostly not good feelings. In her affliction she miscarries, yet she feels relieved because of her doubts. However, that is still not the end of it. In another two weeks, she again has to return to this living nightmare.

FEELING THEIR PAIN

I felt great pain over the challenges these women endured month after month. The best solution I could offer to improve their situation was a combination of Tanya study, meditation, and behavioral modification. I also offered to assist them on the day of their Mikvah immersion and accompany them to the Mikvah. Playing a similar role to that of a midwife, I coached them every step of the way. First, we checked off the list, so I was witness to their adequate preparation. As a result, they stopped spending too much time with their compulsions.

Now, *Baruch Hashem*, these women sufferers leave the Mikvah at ten o'clock and not at midnight. Their *shalom bayit* is positively impacted. Women arrive home from the Mikvah less stressed or embarrassed. Above all, their dignity is restored. When their obsessive thoughts returned, they have someone to turn to, someone to consult, instead of calling the *Rav* in a panic with the same questions, thus adding to her humiliation. These women could reach out for the support they needed whenever they began to doubt if they had done every *bedika* correctly.

At times, when I was out of town or had a speaking engagement, I was unable to be that surrogate helper. I wished I could find a substitute when I was away. I thought about all the women in the world whom I wanted to help. I am just one person. Out of nowhere, a big idea struck me. These women need a specially designed *mikvah* checklist, along with a roster of volunteers to help them until they can get the proper care. I approached a friend of mine with the idea to create a customized checklist designed for OCD, and she discussed it with her friend, who was highly interested in helping with this project. Our checklist was approved by Rabbi S.B. Chaikin and a psychiatrist, Dr. B. Trappler.

I worked with women for months using lessons in Tanya on healing of the mind (more about this in my book *Reaching New Heights through Prayer and Meditation*); Cognitive Behavioral Torah Therapy — staging a rehearsal with them as if they were going to the Mikvah, to get the brain to habituate itself toward desired behaviors — and guided imagery sessions, which is visualizing the successful behaviors. I supported them month after month through the Mikvah preparation process and finally saw these women find their joy. They became far less panicked and had fewer tears, less stress, and less depression. They were laughing and smiling more freely. Eventually, they reached the point where they could go to the Mikvah without help, and even with joy.

They also conceived with joy after years of miscarriages. We smile at the miracle, at the happy mommy holding her precious baby. One day a client of mine said, while holding her baby in her arms, "Miriam this is your baby!" I thought, "Why are you saying this?" Then, as if she could read my mind, she said, "Miriam because of all you have taught me, your help and support I was finally able to conceive after many years of miscarriages!" And again she said, "This baby is your baby." It was one of the best days of my life. I wanted at least 15 children but had medical issues for eight years until G-d blessed me with children.

ADOPT A FRIEND IN NEED

Many women had been on various medications for years, yet they found no relief for their affliction. Others told me that while the medication "took the edge off" of their discomfort, they still felt tormented and were in desperate search of a better solution. With this new program called "Adopt a Friend in Need," these women can get the crucial help they require. All the efforts that have gone into initiating this program are worth all the lives that are saved — the OCD woman herself, her husband, and their future babies. This project is saving the lives of unborn children.

There are those who question whether it is wise to put forth so much effort for the sake of possibly one or two community members. This anecdote brings to mind an encounter between the Lubavitcher Rebbe and Rabbi Gutnick from Australia. In a *yechidus* (audience), the Rebbe asked Rabbi Gutnick to start a *Taharat Hamishpacha* class in his *shul*. The Rabbi answered that he knew his congregants were very interested in *Kabbalah* and mysticism, but not in Family Purity.

"Please do it," said the Rebbe. So the Rabbi, a true *Chassid*, implemented the Rebbe's directive. He paid for advertisements and hired a secretary to phone the congregants. In the end, only one woman came to the class. The Rabbi returned to visit the Rebbe and sadly reported that only one woman showed up. The Rebbe brilliantly answered, "And how many mothers did *Moshe Rabbeinu* have?" If this were the Rebbe's response regarding that program, certainly the Rebbe would encourage us to pursue this program that saves many lives!

The following pages include the Mikvah preparation checklist compiled for women with OCD, approved by Rabbi Sholom Ber Chaikin, a Rav who deals with the laws of family purity, and Dr. Baruch Trappler, a psychiatrist and renowned expert in trauma-research. Special thanks to Mrs. Shulamis Pape and Mikvah.org for their input as well.

Mikvah Preparation Checklist with Suggested Times

Pre-Mikvah Laws and Customs:	Time Allocation	MAXIMUM Time Allocation	Comments
If you must cut your hair, do it three days before			If you cut a small snip on the day of Mikvah, cut away from your body
If you need to shave, do so one day before			If you must shave on the day of Mikvah, be careful not to cut yourself, and check for, and thoroughly wash yourself from, loose hair
If you need to wax, waxing 3 days before is preferable, but 2 days before is okay			Make sure wax is removed
PREPARATIONS:			Use warm water, and soap and shampoo that does not leave a residue
Brush and floss teeth (non-waxed floss is preferable), rinse mouth well (if you usually use other instruments such as a rubber tip or pixie brush, then add time and use it now)	2-3 minutes	4 minutes	
Remove nail polish from fingernails and/or toenails	5 minutes	7 minutes	
Cut and clean nails, fingers and toes: Pay attention to sides with skin overlapping the nail (some use instrument to clean the sides of toe nails). A nailbrush should work for inside and the sides of fingernails. Cut loose skin. If you need to cut a day early because of time restraints it may be allowed, but you must check with a Rav	10 minutes	15 minutes	Rabbi Chaikin says you should cut nails on day of Mikvah. If you cut nails the day before, file them on day of Mikvah. Cut loose skin before you soak.

Suggestion: When washing, start from your head and go downwards in order not to forget anything

Remove all jewelry and makeup, (eyeliner, eye shadow, mascara, lipstick etc.)	7 minutes	10 minutes
Soak body (you can work on your face and finger nails and underarm hair at the same time as you soak)	20 minutes	30 minutes
Wash hair with a mild shampoo that could remove any residue - (Long hair, built-up residue including conditioner require more time for removal)	2 minutes	5 minutes
Eyes - clean inner corners	1 minute	2 minutes
Ears - Pay extra attention to external part that can be seen and remove any leftover cotton from the q-tips. Use a clean earring stick to clean your earring holes	1 minute	2 minutes
Nose - blow and clean	1/2 minute	1/2 minute
Clean other bodily hair well (getting rid of deodorant and/or other residue)	3 minutes	3 minutes
Clean navel with q-tip - (make sure to get out any leftover cotton)	1 minute	2 minutes
Scrub the entire body, paying attention to folds, between the thighs, armpits, areas between fingers and toes and removing glue from band-aids, lotions etc.	5 minutes	6 minutes
Remove artificial teeth etc.	1/2 minute	1/2 minute
Clean vagina internally with warm water	1 minute	1 minute
Make sure there is no soap in nose, ears, mouth or eyes		

Rinse your entire body thoroughly from all soap and shampoo before immersion	3 minutes	4 minutes	
If you go to the bathroom, rewash areas that became soiled	2 minutes	2 minutes	
Comb head hair and separate by hand all other bodily hair (feel for loose hair)	3 minutes	4 minutes	
Check yourself (pay extra attention to your face) and feel areas you cannot see	1 minute	2 minutes	
Remove contact lenses	1 minute	1 minute	Wash hands if necessary
Total time needed to prepare:	1 hour and 10 minutes	1 hour and 42 minutes	

A few tips for immersion:
Be relaxed and hold your lips and eyes gently (not tightly) together
Leave fists unclenched
Feel free to ask the attendants any questions you have
Be happy and feel confident, because Hashem knows you tried

Interventions such as scabs, splinters, blisters etc. should be discussed with a Rav.
Be aware of specifications for Friday or Yom Tov night, and ask your attendant if questions come up at anytime.
Please note: If your personal Rav paskens (decides) differently, there is no need to worry. You can go by his p'sak (decision).

If you have anxiety preparing for the Mikvah, you may be suffering from OCD. You can seek a frum, recommended therapist who can help you. You may also call Rabbi Heller at 718-756-4632, who has helped women deal with questions after Mikvah. Rabbi Heller speaks Yiddish and Hebrew.

Glossary

Bedika: Inspection

Bedi'uk: Precisely

Chametz: Leavening, yeast products (forbidden on Passover)

Chassid: Follower of Chassidism

Chassidus: Chassidism, study of hidden dimension of Torah, emphasizing joy in Jewish prayer and ritual

Chuppah: Marriage canopy

Frum: Religiously observant

Frierdiker Rebbe: The 6th Lubavitcher Rebbe, R' Yosef Yitzchak Schneerson

Halacha: Jewish law

Hashem: G-d

Hayom Yom: An anthology of Chassidic aphorisms and customs arranged by the Rebbe according to the days of the year

Heichal: Courtyard of Holy Temple

Kabbalah: Mystical aspect of Torah

Kavana (ot): Intentions or meditations

Kedusha: Holiness

Ketubah: Marriage contract

Mashpiah: Giver

Mekabel: Receiver

Mikvah: Ritual pool

Mitzvah (ot): Good deed(s), Torah commandment(s)

Moshe Rabbeinu: Moses, our teacher

Moshiach: Messiah

Na'aseh V'nishma: We will do, and we will listen

Nachas: Spiritual/emotional satisfaction

Negal Vasser: Hand washing water

Neshama: Soul

Neshima: Breath

Pesach: Passover

Rambam: Rabbi Moses ben Maimon, commonly known as Maimonides

Rav: Legal decisor

Se'ah: Talmudic measurement of volume

Shabbat: Sabbath

Shalom Bayit: Peace in the home; marital harmony

Shechinah: Holy Spirit

Shofar: Ram's horn blown on Rosh Hashana

Shul: Synagogue

Taharat Hamishpacha: Laws of Family Purity

Tefilla (ot): Prayer(s)

Teshuva: Return

Tikvah: Hope

Toras Emes: Torah of truth

Tumah/Tamei: Impurity/impure

Yechidus: Private audience with the Rebbe

Yetzer Hara: Evil inclination

Acknowledgments

This book is a combined effort of a team of knowledgeable, professional, skilled and talented individuals.

Avigail HaLevy and Chaya Sarah Cantor transcribed many of my classes and helped edit them beautifully and creatively.

Rabbi Michael Seligson always found the time to help identify the many Chassidic sources.

Rivka Zakutinski always helps me forge ahead. Her expertise and helping hand have given me the wherewithal to accomplish many of my goals.

Orah Baer Gerstl, whose encyclopedic knowledge enabled her to catch mistakes not only in the manuscript but in published texts that I cited, and who "fleshed out" the material, clarified the text, and provided footnotes.

The Jewish Girls Unite [JGU] Press Team pulled the pieces together, edited, designed and published the manuscript. Nechama Laber, Manager and Content Editor; Chana Shloush, Copy Editor; Leah Caras, Proofreader and Graphic Designer; Ahuvah Coates organized the material and Sarah Bluming provided insights.

Malka Schwartz, Naomi Bhatia, Suree Ciment, Rivka Vogel and Chana Kaiman who gave insightful and constructive aid.

Special thanks to Rabbi Shloma Majeski for his critique and advice, Mikvah.org and Mrs. Shulamis Pape for reviewing and clarifying the Mikvah laws. Thanks to Reva Baer for proofreading and to Sarah Esther Spielman for editing the OCD article.

May all of you team members be blessed forevermore for all of your enthusiasm, guidance, support and help!

Forever appreciative and grateful to you all!

About the Author

Miriam Yerushalmi holds an MS in Psychology and Family Therapy. She was trained at Pepperdine University and is uniquely skilled at combining behavioral and humanistic approaches to address a wide spectrum of psychopathology.

Miriam fuses essential Torah principles with her background in mental health to offer a unique perspective on essential life issues, ranging from relationships and parenting to self improvement.

Since 2014, Miriam has worked as a counselor for SPARKS (www.sparkscenter.org), a mental health support center for women.

Miriam is a sought after speaker who lectures internationally and has over 250 audio classes available. She lectures for Beis Midrash L'noshim U'banos 770 and has presented at the annual Nefesh conference for therapists. She writes regularly for *The Jewish Press* and *The Jewish Journal*'s "Table For Five," edited by the Accidental Talmudist. She is featured in the course book *What Is?*, a project of the Rohr Jewish Learning Institute (JLI).

Additionally, Miriam has authored a highly acclaimed, multiple-book series called *Reaching New Heights* on marriage, prayer and meditation/mastery of emotional self integration which is endorsed by Dr. Avraham Twersky and Rabbi Shloma Majeski.

She also authored ten children's books helping children better understand themselves and the world around them. Miriam is married with two children and lives in Brooklyn, New York. In addition to leading a non-profit mental health organization, Miriam also has a private practice. She can be reached at miriamyerushalmi18@gmail.com.

Miriam's classes are available on torahanytime.com, torahcafe.com and at bit.ly/ MriamYoutubeChannel.

From Miriam's Clients

The following testimonials were transcribed by Yaacov Dovid Shulman from audio tapes recorded by my clients, and accurately express their words and sentiments. May these stories give hope to others who want to follow these paths as a bridge to happiness.

"I No Longer See Anything Dark in My Life"

I started receiving counseling from Miriam because I had much anger towards my children and my husband. With Miriam's help, I have been learning to be kind to my husband and my children in both my thoughts and words.

Before, I was never really able to feel grateful for what I had. However, now, when I wake up in the morning, the first thing I say is, "I give thanks to my Maker." I am grateful for my husband, for my children, for my house, for the weather. I no longer see anything dark in my life.

Now I can control my emotions. Regarding my relationship with my husband, I started working on myself, and as I changed, he changed too, even though he did not meet with Miriam.

The whole atmosphere in the house has improved. My husband used to complain that he comes home to a house where everybody is screaming and crying. Last night, I opened the door to him with a big smile because I had had a good day. I had received good news that my children are doing well at school. I greeted him with an embrace and began to sing and dance. My children were so happy to see this. When they see me shining, then they glow as well. It's a circle.

"Now My Marriage Is Working Out for the Better"

Miriam taught me not to be needy but to think about what my husband needs. She taught me to be a giver, to look at my husband's actions positively, to forgive and forget, and to tell him what I need instead of blaming him when I lack something. First and foremost, she taught me the importance of connecting myself to G-d and bringing Him into my life in everything that I do. Now my marriage is working out for the better, and I love my husband more.

"My Whole Life Changed"

When I was growing up, my parents and siblings abused me verbally and sometimes physically. I learned not to say anything and to accept the abuse. After I married, that pattern continued. My husband, mother-in-law, sister-in-law, and others mistreated me, and I didn't tell them to stop. When they saw that I didn't defend myself, they continued to put me down.

I became so depressed that my life became unbearable.

I went to therapists and spoke with my rabbi, and they advised me to get a divorce. During this time, many people told me that I have to forgive. I wanted to do so, with all my heart, but I couldn't. I began taking classes with Miriam Yerushalmi. She listened to me, understood me and helped me, and as a result, my depression lifted.

The first thing that she taught me was how to strengthen myself through praying and meditating so that I wouldn't let what other people do depress me. She showed me that the most important way for me to defend myself was to tell someone who is abusing me to stop calmly. However, the most important thing that I learned from Miriam was how to forgive. I learned that if somebody is doing bad things to me, instead of hating them, I should change my feelings and perceptions — for instance, I should feel sorry for that person.

When I learned how to forgive, my whole life changed. This lesson especially changed my marriage. I started everything from the beginning with my husband, exactly as if we had just gotten married.

"My Husband and I Have Never Been Happier"

Miriam is an incredibly warm, talented and compassionate counselor. She is well educated with two degrees in marriage counseling, yet it's her combined utilization of wisdom that brings the miraculous healing results that I experienced. She's gentle, a phenomenal listener, genuinely empathetic, and was able to guide me in my relationship in such a profound fashion that marital issues of over a decade were transformed in a couple of months. Both my husband and I have never been happier in our marriage.

"Miriam Gave Me Back My Hope"

On the advice of others, my spouse and I were divorced. Sometime later, a friend of mine went to Miriam Yerushalmi and suggested that she help us get back together.

Miriam phoned me many times, but I argued that we had been counseled to get a divorce and I refused to consider her help.

Finally, I started going to Miriam to receive her support and counsel; however, I didn't change my mind about the divorce. Then one day, about five months after I had started working with Miriam, I saw my former spouse on the street, walking in my direction. We started talking, and we agreed that about eighty percent of the time our marriage had been pleasant. I said, "If that's the case, then maybe Miriam Yerushalmi could help us out."

After this meeting, I realized how special my spouse was to me: the only one for me, my soulmate without whom I couldn't get along, and with whom I wanted to share my life forever.

However, my former spouse refused to consider our remarrying. I spent a year trying to figure out how to get back together again. I spoke to Miriam Yerushalmi and worked together with her. I read her book, I listened to her CDs, I used her meditations, and I consulted with her, in person and on the telephone. Miriam gave me back my hope. She gave me a positive outlook on how to feel good about myself and my ex and helped me to feel hopeful about the prospect of our getting back together again.

In the meantime, my ex and I slowly started dating, until we finally decided to get married again.

It is important to me to know that Miriam

Yerushalmi is always available to help me. She has been a source of inspiration and has shown me the right path. Miriam's way of delving into deep secrets of how to succeed in marriage, with her woman's touch, has helped me come closer to G-d and, with His help, have a wonderful marriage.

the miraculous healing results that I experienced. She's gentle, a phenomenal listener, genuinely empathetic, and was able to guide me in my relationship in such a profound fashion that marital issues of over a decade were transformed in a couple of months. Both my husband and I have never been happier in our marriage.

"Whoever Crosses Paths with Miriam Yerushalmi Is Blessed"

Miriam Yerushalmi has been in my life for 12 years now. I needed to speak to someone who would help me strengthen my marriage and my commitment to it. Miriam has given me so many tools with which to enhance myself as a person, a wife, and a mother; to be able to deal with whatever comes my way. She has helped me to derive peace and strength from my meditation, to develop patience and the ability to know when to let go — a big asset in clear communication.

Whoever crosses paths with Miriam Yerushalmi is blessed. She is a gift, a unique soul, bringing peace to the world.

"Miriam Helped Me Through This Tough Time"

A few years ago, things were so difficult between my husband and me that I was in total despair and felt that my marriage could not be salvaged.

Miriam helped me through this tough time until I was able to restore my love and respect for my husband and learn to recognize and accept his imperfections as well as my flaws. I learned to be less judgmental and more appreciative of the good things that my husband has brought into our marriage. I am thankful that today I have managed to feel new-found respect for my husband. I can also feel his growing love and respect for me.

Endorsements

"Miriam Yerushalmi is an astounding counselor who has been working for two years with SPARKS, an organization I am very close with which helps women with perinatal depression. She is devoted to helping women in need and is successful in treating them. I believe her book *Reaching New Heights* has a lot of knowledge to offer and will be an inspiring read to all."
Rabbi Dr. Abraham J. Twerski, founder, Gateway Rehabilitation; author of Angels Don't Leave Footprints and many other titles

"As a lecturer for Mikvah USA and as a Mikvah teacher for over 40 years I highly recomend Miriam yerushalmi's Mikvah book Heavenly waters to enhance and deepen the overall Mikvah experience."
-Sarah Karmely, Mikvah teacher

"Mrs Miriam Yerushalmi presents a unique approach which is a beautiful blend of her Chassidic insight and her understanding of human nature. Her ability to see things from a deeper perspective enables her to guide young men and women into improving their personal lives and their marriage in the most challenging of situations. Her determination to keep the family together no matter what, is refreshing in a time when people are getting professional advice in a very different direction. The women that I referred to Miriam for counseling were grateful."
-Rabbi Shloma Majeski, Dean of Machon L' Yahadus

"This book helps connect the seemingly disconnected dots that allow for a clearer picture of you, yourself, your relationships and ultimately, a clearer picture of your best life."
-Judith Leventhal, C.S.W., Author of Small Miracles

"Miriam Yerushalmi is a very successful therapist and an expert on meditation. A part of the SPARKS team, she has conducted deep meditations for women healing from Postpartum Depression and similar mood disorders, enabling them to rebuild their self-image and reconcile past traumas. Her meditations and talks are part of the SPARKS Audio Library, where thousands connect for self-help. As founder and president, I endorse and applaud *Reaching New Heights* series for teaching this valuable technique to all."
-Esther Kenigsberg,
SPARKS founder and president

"I highly recommend *Heavenly Waters*, by Miriam Yerushalmi. Family purity is the foundation of all blessings of married life: *shalom bayit*, healthy children, physical and emotional health, and even financial success. Studying this book, which explains these laws as they relate to mind, body, and spirit, will not only enhance your understanding of this most vital *mitzvah* but will increase the joy of the experience of your Mikvah night."
- Gedale Fenster, Breslov Center of Florida

Other Books by Miriam Yerushalmi

For Adults:

Reaching New Heights Through Kindness in Marriage

Reaching New Heights Through Prayer and Meditation

Reaching New Heights Through Inner Peace Health and Happiness

Reaching New Heights Through Compassionate Parenting (forthcoming)

Reaching New Heights Marriage Workbook (forthcoming)

For Children:

*Feivel the Falafel Ball Who Wanted to Do a Mitzvah**

*Gedalia the Goldfish Who Wanted to Be Like the King**

*Let's Go Camping and Discover Our Nature**

*Beautiful Like a Kallah**

*Carrying a Tune in Tzefat**

*My Best Dress**

Color My Day the Jewish Way

*Let's Go to Eretz Yisrael**

Castle Around My Heart (forthcoming)

Menachem Saves the Day

The Helpful Prince (forthcoming)

*Also in Yiddish and in Hebrew

www.ingramcontent.com/pod-product-compliance
Lightning Source LLC
Chambersburg PA
CBHW060752150426
42811CB00058B/1382

9780578445717